FOOD

AND COOKING IN
17th CENTURY BRITAIN

HISTORY AND RECIPES

First published 1985
by the Historic Buildings and Monuments
Commission for England
© Peter Brears and HBMCE, 1985

Printed by CBE Design & Print, Birmingham
Designed by Elizabeth Mander

C100 10/85
ISBN 1 85074 083 6

FOOD

AND COOKING IN 17th CENTURY BRITAIN

HISTORY AND RECIPES

By Peter Brears

Illustrations by Peter Brears

English ♯ Heritage

Historic Buildings & Monuments Commission for England

THE
LAMENTABLE
COMPLAINTS
OF
NICK FROTH the Tapfter, and
RULEROST the Cooke.

*Concerning the reftraint lately fet forth,
against drinking, potting, and piping on the Sab-
bath day, and against felling meate.*

*In this broadside of 1641,
the tapster and the cook complain of
the new regulations which prevent them from trading on Sundays.
Note the cook's 'lusty surloins of roast Beefe'
turning in front of the fire*

INTRODUCTION

he seventeenth century was a period of tremendous upheaval and change in this country, a period in which virtually every aspect of our national and domestic life was transformed as England cast off many of her medieval traditions to emerge as a new, forward-looking state. As a result of the dissolution of the monasteries in the 1530s, vast areas of land and previously untapped economic resources had passed into lay hands. As they were enthusiastically developed over the succeeding century, their growing productivity financed the rise of what was to be a new, prosperous and influential class – the landed gentry.

In an age when the sovereign sturdily maintained his Divine Right to govern as he wished, it was impossible for the gentry to obtain the political power they now sought, the friction generated between these opposing views flaring up into the Civil Wars which terminated in the execution of Charles I in 1649. After just a decade of puritanical Commonwealth government, England returned to monarchy with Charles II in 1660. Now it was a constitutional monarchy, however, one which recognized the right of Parliament to play a leading role in managing the country's affairs.

These upheavals had a considerable effect on domestic life. From the early 1600s the increasing affluence of the gentry had enabled them to spend much more on recreation, travel and luxury goods. Instead of living throughout the year on their quiet estates, they now spent long periods in the towns, visits to London allowing them to acquire all manner of social graces. Here they might participate in advantageous parliamentary, commercial or legal business, perhaps take fencing or dancing lessons, use the services of fine tailors and wig-makers, or enjoy excursions to the theatre, musical events, great houses, or the court. In the 1620s, proclamations ordered the gentry to return to their estates to prevent the neglect of public duties, avoidance of tax and the heavy expenditure on foreign luxuries and expensive foods. These were largely ignored, however, and lavish entertainment flourished during the London season, as the city continued to develop as the finest food market in the kingdom.

Up to this time the fare of the country gentleman had been relatively plain and simple, largely based on home-produced meat, game and grain, roasted, boiled or baked as required. Plenty had been preferred to variety, but now there was an increasing demand for new delicacies, with new flavours and new methods of cookery. As in all aspects of social life, the royal household set the required fashions and standards of culinary taste, drawing both on its own centuries-old traditions and on new developments from France. Dishes which appeared at court would be imitated in lesser households, and thus proceed on down the social scale, their recipes probably being passed on at dinner or supper parties. At these functions the ladies would also exchange recipes for their own specialities, together with those culled from the ever-increasing range of cookery books. Between 1600 and 1700 a new volume appeared almost every other year, the most popular of these often running into a number of editions. With titles such as *The English Hus-wife, The Accomplish'd Lady's Delight,* or *The Genteel House-Keeper's Pastime,* they appear to have been primarily intended for use in prosperous families, where the lady of the house was responsible for all aspects of housekeeping. Many of the recipes were individually attributed to the royal kitchens, or to ladies of the court, which presumably gave them a certain socially prestigious cachet. These volumes contained many items from overseas, such as 'a Persian Dish', 'a Turkish Dish', 'a Portugal Dish', or even 'an Outlandish Dish', but France provided the most fertile source of new recipes. In the late sixteenth century Sir Hugh Platt had published some 'after the French fashion', while John Murrell's *New Booke of Cookerie* of 1617 was 'all set forth according to the now new English and French Fashion'. F.P. de La Varenne's *Cuisinier françois,* published in Paris in 1651, was to have the greatest influence, particularly after it was 'English'd by J.G.D.' and appeared as *The French Cook* in London in 1653. It included recipes for hash, and for dishes both 'a la daube' and 'a la mode'. By 1688

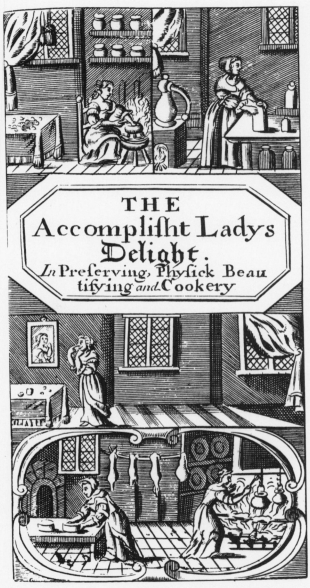

THE
Accomplisht Ladys
Delight.
In Preserving, Physick Beau
tifying and Cookery

The frontispiece of The Accomplisht Lady's Delight *of 1677 shows ladies busily preserving, distilling, making cosmetics, and working in the kitchen*

cooks' glossaries included a wide range of newly introduced French terms, including:

A-la-Sauces Sauce made after the French Almaigne or German fashion.

A-la-Doode is a French way of ordering any large Fowl or Leg of Mutton.

A-la-Mode way is the new, or French way of dressing all manner of boiled or baked Meat.

Bouillon is a kind of Broth or boiled meat made of several things.

Hash is a Dish-meat made of any kind flesh minced or in Gobbets stewed in strong broth with spices, and served up in a Dish with Sippets: to Hash is to stew any Meat that is cold. The French call it Hach or Hachee.

Hautgoust a thing that hath an high taste, viz. a Ho-goo.

Salmagundi an Italian dish [actually from France] made of cold turkey and other Ingredients.

Although a number of new dishes were introduced from other European countries, such as Italy's macaroni, vermicelli and 'tortelleti', and Spain's olla podrida (an amazing variety of stewed meats and vegetables, anglicized to 'hotch-potch'), the French influence was predominant. Even so, it did not overwhelm the native English taste for good plain cooking. Many still preferred substantial, solid, wholesome roast and boiled meats, to the highly priced Frenchified

Hogg-podg Dish-meats, neither pleasing to the Pallet, or of credit to the Masters... But let Cooks study new Dish-meats and work out their Brains, when they have done all they can, there are but four sorts of Meat which they can properly, and with safety, work upon, viz. Flesh of Beasts, Flesh of Fowle, Flesh of Fish and Field Fruits; and these again are according to their kinds either Stewed, Boiled, Parboiled, Fryed, Broiled, Roasted, Baked, Hashed, Pickled, Souced, or made into Sweet-Meats. Nil Ultra.

Ingredients

By the opening of the seventeenth century, most of our present-day foodstuffs had already been introduced. The English countryside, parks and farms were producing venison and all other kinds of game, mutton, pork, and beef, while increasing quantities of beef were also being imported from Scotland. Ever since the Union of the Crowns in 1603, great herds of black cattle had been driven south over the border, slowly working their way down to London, beasts being sold off at fairs en route. On all but the poorest tables, meat often formed some three-quarters of every meal. Much of this was freshly killed, but various techniques of salting and potting enabled it to be preserved for use throughout the winter months.

Most vegetables grown today were already known, ranging from cabbages, savoy, kale, cauliflower and broccoli, to carrots, turnips, parsnips and beetroot, artichokes, onions, peas and beans. Common (or sweet), Virginian and Canadian potatoes were grown here too, but they were still regarded as a novelty. The interest in gardening which had started in the later sixteenth century continued to expand; orchards and gardens now yielded a wealth of fruit, in addition to lettuce, chicory, celery, cucumbers and radishes. The medieval suspicion of raw vegetables and fruit was slowly subsiding, and salads were beginning to appear on the table with increasing frequency. In 1699 John Evelyn even published a whole book on the subject, *Acetaria, a Discourse of Sallets,* in which he suggested a dressing made of three parts of olive oil, one part vinegar, lemon or orange juice, dry mustard, and mashed hard-boiled egg yolks.

New foodstuffs imported from overseas during this period included allspice or Jamaica pepper from the West Indies, cochineal from Mexico, and sago from Malaya. From the 1640s, when the English colonists in Barbados turned their land over to sugar cane, sugar became much more plentiful, leading to a great increase in the production of homemade preserves, confectionery and syrups. The most significant group of new foods, however, were all beverages. By the 1660s it was possible to purchase in London: 'That excellent and by all Physitians approved China drink called by the Chineans Tcha, by other nations Tay alias Tee', 'Coffa, which is a blacke kind of drinke made of a kind of Pulse like Pease, called Coaus', which came from Arabia and Turkey, and chocolate, from the West Indies. Despite complaints that these novel drinks would damage the trade in home-grown barley and malt, in addition to making men 'as unfruitful as the deserts', they all enjoyed a popularity which has continued unabated up to the present day.

In addition to these new and exotic dishes, great strides were being made in the use of traditional home-grown produce. This was most clearly seen in bakery, where a whole host of significant developments were taking place. The 'great cakes' of the medieval period, enriched with butter, cream, eggs and sugar, heavily fruited and spiced, raised with yeast, and weighing twenty pounds or more, continued to be popular for important occasions. Now they were contained within a tinplate hoop, however, thus making them much more convenient both to bake and to serve. One new variety was the Banbury cake. Specially baked for wedding feasts, its outer layer of plain dough concealed a rich filling of dough mingled with currants. It was in this period too that the modern baked gingerbread appeared, this somewhat sticky sponge, flavoured with ginger and cinnamon, replacing the earlier solid paste of highly spiced breadcrumbs and wine.

Biscuits went through a similar transformation. The medieval biscuit had been made by dusting slices of an enriched bread roll with sugar and spices before returning them to the oven where they hardened into a kind of sweet rusk. By baking the biscuit-bread in the form of a single light, finely-textured loaf, it changed into sponge cake. This was often entitled 'fine cake' in contemporary recipe books. Other new varieties of biscuit included both jumbals, where caraway-flavoured dough was worked up into interlaced rings, knots, or plaits, and Shrewsbury cakes whose rounds of shortcake were perhaps spiced with ginger or cinnamon.

As baking skills developed throughout England, some areas acquired a reputation for their own local specialities. This was particularly true of a number of northern towns, Chorley, Eccles, Dewsbury and Halifax giving their names to distinct variations of the currant pasty.

'BLESSED BE HE THAT INVENTED PUDDING', wrote M Misson in the 1690s; 'Ah, what an excellent thing is an English pudding!' Savoury black and white puddings forced into animal guts had been made for generations, but the early seventeenth century saw the development of that great English invention, the pudding cloth. Utilizing this simple device, it was possible to convert flour, milk, eggs, butter, sugar, suet, marrow and raisins, etc. into a whole series of hot, filling and nutritious dishes with minimal time, trouble and cost. Having securely tied the ingredients within the cloth, the pudding had only to be plunged into a boiling pot, perhaps along with the meat and vegetables, where it could simmer for hours without further attention. Varying in texture and quality from light, moist custards to substantial masses of heavily fruited oatmeal, the boiled pudding soon became a mainstay of English cookery, being adopted by all sections of society.

Further puddings or 'pudding pies' were poured into dishes and baked in the oven. Rice puddings were readily made in this way, as were whitepots, the luxurious predecessors of bread-and-butter pudding.

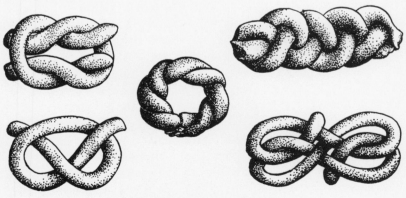

Designs for 'Knotts or Gumballs'

Equipment

In the kitchens of the seventeeth century, activity centred around broad-arched fireplaces recessed into the walls, each measuring at least six feet wide by a yard in depth. Here great log fires supported on firedogs, or coal fires raised within elevated wrought-iron baskets, provided all the heat necessary for boiling and roasting. Boiling was one of the most economical ways of cooking, cauldrons of iron or brass suspended over the fire being employed to heat whole meals in a single operation. Joints of meat could be plunged into the boiling water, together with vegetables contained in net bags, or puddings either tied up in cloths or floating in wooden bowls, there to remain until thoroughly cooked. As an alternative, poultry, game or small quantities of meat could be placed in an earthenware vessel, with butter, herbs and spices, a lid sealed in place with a strip of pastry, and the vessel immersed in the cauldron for a few hours. In this

Cauldron cookery: here a pot containing meat, butter and herbs simmers with vegetables and a pudding

Roasting a pig

way, richly flavoured and tender dishes were produced, including jugged hare, in which the jointed animal was cooked within a jug.

A similar principle was employed in one of the most ingenious culinary inventions of this period, the pressure-cooker or 'digester'. Denys Papin, a French physicist and mathematician living in London, discovered that most foodstuffs could be efficiently cooked in a totally sealed vessel, thus making considerable savings in time, fuel and flavour. To demonstrate the advantages of this method, he invited a number of fellow-members of the Royal Society to join him for a supper in April 1682, at which 'all was dressed, both fish and flesh, in digesters, by which the hardest bones were made as soft as cheese, without water or other liquor, and with less than eight ounces of coals, producing an incredible quantity of gravy, but nothing exceeded the pigeons, which tasted just as if baked in a pie, all these being stewed in their own juice, without any addition of water save what swam about the digester.' As with so many other improvements, centuries were to pass before these advantages were fully appreciated, and pressure-cooking finally became an everyday method of preparing meat, fish and vegetables for the table.

For roasting, meat was mounted on long iron spits or 'broaches' supported on spit dogs or cobirons. Here it could be rotated before the fire, probably for four or five hours in the case of a large joint. For the turnspit, the youth employed to turn the spit, it was a laborious, boring and uncomfortable job, his front being roasted by the heat of the fire while his back was chilled by the cold draughts which rushed forward to fan the flames. It is not surprising that this was the first domestic process to be fully mechanized. From the early seventeenth century weight-driven clockwork jacks mounted on the sides of the fireplaces were increasingly used to turn the spits at a slow and uniform rate. In some kitchens dog-power was preferred. Doctor Caius, founder of Caius College, Cambridge, stated that: 'There is comprehended under the curs of the coarsest kind a certain dog in kitchen service excellent. For when any meat is to be roasted, they go into a wheel, which they turning about with the weight of their bodies, so diligently look to their business, that no drudge or scullion can do the meat more cunningly, whom the popular sort hereupon term turnspits.'

Turning the meat was only one of the tasks involved in roasting. Even before it was secured on to the spit, game and poultry had to be cleaned and trussed, while sucking pigs required more detailed attention. Having made sure that the mouth was wedged open before rigor mortis set in, this most succulent of roasts was mounted on the spit, stuffed with bread and herbs such as sage, sewn up, and then placed before the fire. As roasting proceeded, the drops of fat issuing from the meat were caught in a long shallow dripping pan whose sloping base conducted them into a central well. From here they could be taken up with a basting ladle and poured back over the meat, to keep it moist and tender.

For heating smaller quantities of food, saucepans were made of iron, bronze, tinned copper, or silver. As they were difficult to use over the open fires, they were supported either on a brigg, a horizontal framework bridging the topmost firebars, or on a trivet, a tall three-legged iron stand which stood in front of the fire to take advantage of the radiant heat. Alternatively, a shorter version of the trivet, called a brandreth, could hold a pan just a few inches above the gentle heat of a small fire burning on the hearth. Skillets and posnets were also used in this position, their pan-like bodies being raised on three integral legs.

In large establishments, where entertainment was provided on a lavish scale, the kitchen usually housed a stove in addition to the normal fireplace. This took the form of a long masonry bench built against a wall, usually being placed close to a window to ensure adequate ventilation. Its working surface was pierced by a number of iron-sheathed fire baskets, their bases being separated from open flues below by series of closely spaced firebars. Once filled with

A weight-driven clockwork jack, used to turn the spit before the fire

glowing charcoal, the stove provided a clean and easily controlled heat, ideal for making sauces, preserves or many made dishes.

The only other cooking facility to be found in the seventeenth-century kitchen was the bee-hive oven. This was a circular domed construction, measuring perhaps three feet or more in diameter, built into the thickness of one of the walls and entered by way of a small square doorway. The equipment and methods used in baking bread, one of the major tasks in any household, are clearly described in Randle Holme's *Academy of Armory* of 1688. Using a meal shovel *(1)* the baker first transferred a batch of flour from a large storage chest or ark into a plank-built kneading trough *(2)*. Here it was blended with warm water, salt or spices, and yeast which had been made by dissolving a piece of old sour dough in water. The soft dough was then removed from the trough, using a dough scraper *(3)*, and transferred to the brake *(4)*, a strong table fitted with a long hinged roller with which the dough was kneaded and beaten until ready for moulding. On the moulding table *(5)* a dough knife *(6)* measuring about two feet in length was used to divide the dough so that it could be weighed and moulded into loaves or rolls. After the loaf had been cut, by

Illustrated in Randle Holme's Academy of Armory *of 1688, these bakers' tools include 1 a meal shovel, 2 a kneading trough, 3 a dough scraper, 4 a brake, 5 a moulding table, 6 a dough knife, 7 an oven, 8 a kid of gorse on a pitchfork, 9 a peel, and 10 a custard filler*

running the knife around the sides, and pricked across the top with a sharp bodkin, it was stamped with the baker's name or mark so that it could be readily identified if found faulty or short in weight.

It was now ready for the oven *(7)*. This had been fired to a high temperature by thrusting a burning kid of gorse into its chamber, using a short pitch fork *(8)*. When the oven was up to temperature, the fire and ashes were swept out, and the loaves slipped inside using a long-handled peel *(9)*. Once the oven had been sealed with a slab of stone, set in place with clay or dirt out of the street, the heat remaining in the masonry slowly baked the bread to perfection. Having broken away the mud which sealed the door, the oven was opened and the bread drawn out on the peel. As there was still a considerable quantity of heat left in the oven, further items of bakery, such as puddings, pasties and pies which required longer low-temperature cooking, were then inserted. If custards were being made, their blind pastry cases were now put in and filled almost to the brim with a sweet egg and milk mixture poured from a long-handled wooden custard filler *(10)*. The door was then sealed in place again and the contents left to bake for the required time. If further baking was required, the whole process had to be repeated, reheating the oven with more gorse, cleaning out the hot embers, etc. It is not surprising that the first iron ovens which were able to provide a constant source of heat proved to be so successful when introduced in the eighteenth century.

In the kitchens of the royal household, and in those of leading members of the court, the cooks had to develop new skills from the early 1660s, when ice-cream began to be made in this country. By constructing straw-thatched ice-houses or snow-pits, dug deep into the ground, it was now possible to keep stocks of winter ice throughout the year. When ice-cream was required, blocks of ice were brought into the kitchen, broken into lumps, and packed around a small metal pan containing sweetened cream, perhaps flavoured with orange flower water. Having been left to freeze for a couple of hours, it was then turned out on to a salver and sent up to the table, where it formed an interesting delicacy for the banquet course.

Table setting, c.1660

Tableware

p to the opening decades of the seventeenth century the gentry had lived within large households, usually thirty or more in number, including relations, chaplains, tutors, porters and a large number of servants. In all but the grandest houses, they all dined together in the great hall. The master and his chief guests sat at the top table, probably raised on a dais surmounted by a tall canopy, while the remainder occupied tables below, in the body of the hall. When the gentry started to spend more time in town, and more money on personal pleasures, the old-fashioned extended household proved to be an expensive encumbrance, and soon became a thing of the past.

Imitating the Elizabethan nobility, the gentry now abandoned the great hall for all but the largest social events, and began to take their meals in a completely new setting – the dining room. In older houses, the parlour, a private bed-sitting room, was often transformed into a dining room, with new decorations and furniture, while in new houses a good-quality purpose-built dining room was of the greatest importance. With its walls lined with elegant timber panelling or embossed, painted and gilded Cordovan goatskin, its plaster ceiling enriched with mouldings and robustly-modelled ornament, its impressive fireplace and curtained windows, the dining room provided an ideal setting in which to entertain guests, and make a powerful display of wealth and taste.

From the middle of the century, dining rooms were being furnished with a dining table, often of the oval gate-legged variety, surrounded by a matching set of chairs for the most important diners. There might also be a long table and a set of stools for other members of the household, while livery cupboards or sideboards would be provided both to hold dishes of food and to display vessels of gold, silver or fine pottery.

When preparing the table, it was first covered with a fine linen cloth, probably woven with a damask design. Over this, the table was laid with all the required plates, salts, casters and saucers. These were made of silver or silver-gilt in the larger houses, for they provided a convenient and ostentatious means of storing one's wealth in a period when modern banking systems were still in their infancy. Much early plate was melted down during the Civil War, but from the Restoration there was a great revival in the use of silver tableware, which now appeared in a whole range of new and robustly elegant designs. In 1670, for example, Prince Rupert purchased five dozen silver plates from Alderman Blackwell, each plate weighing 17¾ ounces at 5s 8d per ounce, the whole set costing almost £300. This gives some indication of the high costs involved in furnishing a table with good-quality silverware. Much of this domestic plate was made in London, where it found a ready market among the nobility and gentry who came up to town for the winter season, but major regional centres such as Newcastle, York, Chester, Norwich and Exeter also produced silverware of the highest standard.

Since solid silver was extremely expensive, many households used pewter as a substitute. Composed of tin, with a small percentage of lead and copper, this metal cost only 1s to 1s 2d a pound, and therefore could be used in much greater quantities by

Earthenware drinking vessels in 'jewelled' and feathered Staffordshire slipware, 1690, in black-glazed redware from Potovens near Wakefield c.1680, in tin-glaze decorated with blue brushwork, made in Southwark in 1633, and a brown salt-glazed stoneware mug probably made in Nottingham by James Morley, c.1700

On this fine Staffordshire charger by Thomas Toft, Charles II makes an appropriately loyal image for the multi-coloured slipware decoration

a far wider section of the community. When brightly polished, it closely resembled silver, but it was much softer. Even a moderately hard cut with a knife would score its surface quite deeply, so that it was in need of constant maintenance, the marks received at table either burnished over, or polished out using fine abrasive sand.

This troublesome operation could be avoided by using delftware made of a light biscuit-coloured pottery covered in a smooth and glossy opaque white glaze. Having been made in England from the 1560s, it now enjoyed great popularity, its production being centred in the London parishes of Aldgate and Southwark and, from the mid-seventeenth century, at Brislington near Bristol. Many pieces were decorated with blue brushwork in the Chinese manner, imitating Ming or 'Transitional' porcelain, while others, particularly the large 'blue-dash chargers' (so-called from the decoration around their rims), were painted with brightly coloured flowers, portraits, or pictures of Adam and Eve. English lead-glazed earthenware also made great advances from the mid-seventeenth century, particularly in the manufacture of tableware. By the 1660s, the supremacy of the Staffordshire potters had already become fully established, their slipwares decorated in coloured liquid clays being particularly attractive. The great dishes of Thomas Toft, with their lively royal portraits or coats of arms, provided appropriately loyal images for the dining room.

In many households, wooden tableware was still in use, the square wooden trencher, with a large hollow for meat and a small hollow for salt, now being replaced by circular wooden plates or platters. Large communal drinking bowls still survived too, but from the end of Elizabeth's reign glassware had become much more common, appearing in the form of wine glasses, tumblers, and an excellent range of sweetmeat, jelly and syllabub glasses.

The most significant change in tableware was the introduction of the fork. Forks had been used for eating sweetmeats on royal and noble tables since the fourteenth century, but they only emerged as a major item of cutlery from the early seventeenth century, when they were popularized by Thomas Coryat. He published an account of their use in Italy in 1611, while in 1616 Ben Jonson asked

'Forks! what be they?'
'The laudable use of forks,
Brought into custom here, as they are in Italy,
To the sparing of napkins.'

Half a century was to pass before they were generally accepted, however, but by the 1660s sets of knives and forks were being made, the knife now adopting a rounded end, in contrast to its earlier pointed form which had been necessary when it had to spear meat from the dishes.

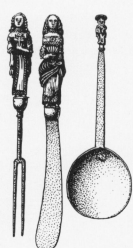

Dating from the 1660s, the knife and fork are of steel with carved ivory handles, while the spoon is of solid silver, with a gilt knop

The Meals

At this period the day was punctuated by three main meals; breakfast, taken shortly after rising, dinner, taken at midday, and supper, taken in the early evening. The first of these was a relatively light meal by the standards of the day, probably having a selection of cold meats, bread and butter, and cakes served with tea, coffee or chocolate by the end of the century. Then as now, there were great contrasts in breakfast preferences, however, the Cromwells taking rich broth or caudle, followed by a cup of small ale with toast and sugar at mid-morning.

Unlike today's dinners, in which the frequent courses follow each other in a set sequence from soup to dessert, the seventeenth-century dinner was only of two or, at most, three courses. Each course comprised a number of diverse dishes, including both sweets and savouries, so that the diner could help himself to whatever he liked in the manner of a modern buffet, thus giving each individual a much greater freedom of choice. The first course would be placed on the table in a neat, symmetrical arrangement, and include most of the major meat dishes, together with soups which would be removed and their place taken by a further dish once everyone had been served. In the second course there would be a range of lighter meats, game and sweet stuff laid in a similar symmetrical pattern, but this division of the dishes was only a general rule, leaving plenty of scope to include whatever might be available at any particular time.

The third course was composed of fruit, sweets and cheese, but the manner in which it was served changed as the century progressed. In the earlier decades, it continued the popular Elizabethan practice of banqueting; the 'banquet' in this case being an elaborate dessert course of sweetmeats etc. served either as a meal in itself or as a continuation of dinner or supper, usually set out in a separate apartment. It presented an opportunity for the cooks and the gardeners to make a great show of their skills, with elaborate confections and rare fruits displayed in new and exciting

James I and the young Prince Henry entertaining the Spanish Ambassador.
Note the plate, knife and manchet bread-roll set before each diner,
the arrangement of the dishes on the table, and the two standing salts

ways. For important functions, cardboard galleons sailing on seas
of salt could startle guests with their cannon, fired with real
gunpowder, while pastry deer bled red wine when arrows were
pulled from their sides.

John Evelyn gives the following colourful account of
William and Mary's entertainment for the Venetian ambassadors,
when 'the banquet was twelve vast chargers piled up so high that
those that sat one against another could hardly see each other. Of
these sweetmeats, which doubtless took some days piling up in this
exquisite manner, the Ambassadors touched not, but left them to
the spectators… in a moment of time all that curious work was
demolished, the confitures voided, and the tables cleared.' This
appears to have been the fate of many royal banquets. Even when
the Garter knights held their great dinner in the magnificent
Banqueting House in Whitehall, 'the banqueting-stuff was flung

around the room profusely.' In most households, however, particularly from the Restoration, the third course began to be served at the dining table, in the manner of a modern dessert.

At supper, early in the evening, only a single course was laid, but it could be made up of numerous dishes, or be extended by a banquet whenever necessary. Then, after a few hours of good conversation, music, singing or cards, accompanied by much alcohol and perhaps tobacco, the company would be served with a light meal to prepare them either for their homeward journey or for the chill of the bedroom – Pepys, for example, having 'a good sack-posset and cold meat and sent my guests away about 10 a-clock at night'. The sack posset certainly provided the ideal close to the day. Made of eggs, wine and spices scalded with sweetened cream, spooned from the most beautifully decorated silverware, or sipped from voluminous earthenware vessels, its rich smooth warmth and alcoholic potency soon lulled the diners into total oblivion: 'And so to bed.'

This London silver posset pot was purchased by John Hutton of Marske in 1669 to celebrate the birth of his son and heir

*In this broadside of 1641, Mistress Abel
fixes a chicken on the spit in her kitchen at
'The Ship', Old Fish Street, in London*

RECIPES

The recipes have been chosen to demonstrate a typical range of seventeenth-century dishes, and to give some impression of their diverse flavours. They include some of the newly introduced varieties of pudding and bakery, in addition to contemporary versions of well-established foods.

First and second courses for a meal may be made up from a combination of any of the meat dishes with a pudding and either hot or cold roasts; while the various sweets, cakes and biscuits, with fresh fruit and cheese, can form a banquet or third course. As an alternative, any of the recipes can be used individually as part of an otherwise modern meal.

DIET BREAD

The receypte of the Dyett bread: Take halfe a pecke of Fyne Wheaten Flower, three handfull of sage shredd small, An ounce and a halfe of ordinary Fennell seede lightly bruised, strawe the sage and the Fennell seede amongst the Flower, and so with barme kneade and bake ytt as you do other breade, and eate ytt nott untill ytt be a day old.

14 oz (400 g) plain flour
2 tbls (30 ml) dried sage
½ oz (15 g) fennel seed, bruised
½ oz (15 g) dried yeast mixed with 1 tsp
(5ml) sugar and ½ pt (275 ml)
warm water

Mix the dry ingredients in a warm bowl, make a well in the centre, work in the liquid, knead, and leave to rise in a warm place for 1 hour. Knead the dough on a floured board, shape into a round cob or a number of small cakes, and allow to prove for 15 minutes before baking at gas mark 8, 450°F (230°C) for 15 minutes, and then for a further 40 minutes at gas mark 6, 400°F (200°C). This bread has a delicate aniseed flavour, and makes an interesting accompaniment to soups, fish or cheese.

A Temple Newsam recipe quoted in The Gentlewoman's Kitchen

DUTCH PUDDING

Take a pound and a halfe of Fresh Beef, all lean, take a pound and a quarter of Beef Suet, sliced both very small, then take a half-penny stale Loaf and grate it, a handfull of Sage and a little Winter Savory, a little Time, shred these very small; take four Eggs, half a pint of Cream, a few Cloves, Nutmegs, Mace and Pepper, finely beaten, mingle them all together very well, with a little Salt; roll it all up together in a green Colwort Leaf, and then tye it up hard in a Linnen-Cloth, garnish your Dish with grated bread and serve it up with mustard in Saucers.

12 oz (350 g) coarsely minced lean beef
8 oz (225 g) suet
4 oz (125 g) dry breadcrumbs
2 tsps (10 ml) dried sage
1 tsp (5 ml) dried savory
1 tsp (5 ml) dried thyme
2 eggs
¼ tsp (1.5 ml) ground cloves
¼ tsp (1.5 ml) grated nutmeg
¼ tsp (1.5 ml) ground mace
¼ tsp (1.5 ml) pepper
2 tsps (10 ml) salt
1-2 large cabbage leaves
fresh breadcrumbs, to garnish
made English mustard, to serve

Mix all the ingredients together and form into a round ball. Wrap in a large cabbage leaf, and tie up tightly in a linen cloth. Plunge into boiling water, and simmer for 2 hours. To serve, turn out of the cloth on to a bed of fresh breadcrumbs, accompanied by a saucer of English mustard. The dish looks just like a cabbage at this stage, but may be carved with ease.

Elizabeth Cromwell: The Court and Kitchen of Mrs Elizabeth Commonly called Joan Cromwell

SCOTCH COLLOPS

To Make Scotch Collops: R. a legge of Mutton, cutt itt in round pieces as broad as you can, & the thickness of a thin halfe-crowne, fry them in sweet butter very browne, but not too hard, then take four or five spoonfull of Clarett-wine, two spoonfull of vinegar, an onion slit, halfe a nuttmegge grated, Lemon-pill, an Anchovee, a little horse-radish, & oysters if you have them, putt all into the Frying-pan together with the meat, & a quarter of a pound of butter beaten thick, tosse them in the Pan a while over the fire, but do not let them boyle, then heat your dish, rubb it with Shallot or garlick, & send them upp quick.

1 lb (450 g) lean lamb or mutton
6 oz (175 g) butter
5 tbls (75 ml) claret
2 tbls (30 ml) vinegar
1 onion
2 anchovy fillets
1 tbls (15 ml) horseradish sauce
1 garlic clove

Thinly slice the meat, and stir fry gently with half the butter for 5-10 minutes until browned. Remove from the heat, and add all the remaining ingredients, except for the garlic. Heat gently for a few minutes, stirring the pan continuously, until almost at boiling point. Slice the garlic, and rub it around the inside of the serving dish before pouring in the collops. Serve immediately. This is an excellent way of making a rich and full-flavoured meat dish in a very short time.

The Savile Recipe Book, 1683, quoted in The Gentlewoman's Kitchen

---

SALAD

For the salad:
young leaves of lettuce, sorrel, mustard, cress, dandelion, spinach, radishes
8 oz (225 g) capers
12 dates, sliced lengthways
2 oz (50 g) raisins
2 oz (50 g) currants
2 oz (50 g) blanched almonds
6 figs, sliced
6 mandarin oranges, peeled and divided into segments

For the decoration:
5 small branches of rosemary
4 lemons
8 oz (225 g) fresh or glacé cherries
6 hard-boiled eggs

Mix the contents of the salad together (reserving half the capers, dates, almonds and oranges for decoration) and spread evenly across a wide shallow dish. Spike each branch of rosemary into the pointed end of five half-lemons, and hang with the cherries before placing one in the centre of the salad, and the remaining four equidistant around it. Prick four half-eggs with the reserved almonds and dates, both sliced lengthways, and place these between the four half-lemons. Quarter the remaining eggs, and alternate with slices of lemon just within the brim of the dish. Then decorate the brim with alternating orange segments and small piles of capers.

The Second Book of Cookery

A 'Grand Sallet' of 1641

BRAWN

To bake Brawne: Take two Buttocks and hang them up two or three dayes, then take them down and dip them into hot-water, and pluck off the skin, dry them very well with a clean Cloth, when you have so done, take Lard, cut it in pieces as big as your little finger, and season it very well with Pepper, Cloves, Mace, Nutmeg, and Salt, put each of them into an earthen Pot, put in a pint of Claret-wine, a pound of Mutton Suet. So close it with paste, let the Oven be well heated, and so bake them, you must give them time for the baking according to the bigness of the Haunches and the thickness of the Pots, they commonly allot seven hours for the baking of them; let them stand three days, then take off the Covers, and pour away all the liquor, then have clarified butter, and fill up both the Pots to keep it for use, it will very well keep two or three months.

2-3 lb (900 g–1.4 kg) joint of lean
  pork
½ bottle (350 ml) claret
2 oz (50 g) suet
2 tsps (10 ml) salt
½ tsp (2.5 ml) ground mace
¼ tsp (1.5 ml) pepper
¼ tsp (1.5 ml) ground cloves
¼ tsp (1.5 ml) grated nutmeg
shortcrust pastry made with
  4 oz (125 g) plain flour and
  2 oz (50 g) lard

Trim any fat or rind from the joint, and cut into strips. Truss the joint tightly, place in a deep casserole, then add the strips of fat and the remaining ingredients except for the pastry. Roll out the pastry, and use it to cover the casserole, carefully sealing the edges. Bake at gas mark 4, 350°F (180°C) for 2½ hours, then leave in a cool place overnight. Remove the crust, lift out the joint, wipe clean, and carve as required. The remaining stock can be used to provide a highly-flavoured basis for soups etc.

Rebecca Price: The Compleat Cook

A cast bronze skillet of 1684

CHICKEN CULLIS

To make a cullis as white as snowe and in the nature of gelly: Take a cocke, scalde, wash and draw him clene, seeth it in white wine or rhenish wine, skum it cleane, clarifie the broth after it is strained, then take a pinte of thicke & sweet creame, straine that to your clarified broth, and your broth will become exceeding faire and white; then take powdred ginger, fine white sugar and Rosewater, seething your cullis when you season it, to make it take the colour the better.

1 chicken
1½ pt (850 ml) white wine or white
   wine and water
1 egg white, lightly beaten
1 pt (575 ml) single cream
½ tsp (2.5 ml) ground ginger
2 tbls (30 ml) sugar
1 tbls (15 ml) rosewater

Simmer the chicken in the wine, or wine and water, until tender – about 45-50 minutes. Remove the chicken from the pan and keep it hot, ready for the table. Beat the egg white into the stock, and continue to whisk over a moderate heat until it comes to the boil. Stop whisking immediately and allow the liquid to rise to the top of the pan before removing it from the heat for a few minutes to allow the fine particles to form a soft curd with the egg white. Pour the liquid through a fine cloth into a clean pan, place on a gentle heat, and stir slowly while pouring in the cream. Heat the cullis almost to boiling point, stirring continuously, and finally add the ginger, sugar and rosewater just before serving.

The cullis may be poured over the chicken resting on crustless cubes of white bread, in a deep dish. Alternatively, it can be served separately as a soup, when its smooth texture and rich, delicate flavour can be enjoyed to the full.

Sir Hugh Platt: Delightes for Ladies

KNOT BISCUITS

*To make Knotts or Gumballs: Take 12
Yolkes of Egges, & 5 Whites, a pound
of searced Sugar, half a pound of
Butter washed in Rose Water, 3
quarters of an ounce of Mace finely
beaten, a little Salt dissolved in Rose
Water, half an ounce of Caroway-seeds,
Mingle all theise together with as much
Flower as will worke it up in paste, &
soe make it Knotts or Rings or What
fashion you please. Bake them as
Bisket-bread, but upon Pye-plates.*

1½ oz (40 g) butter
1 tbls (15 ml) rosewater
4 oz (100 g) sugar
2 eggs, beaten
1 tsp (5 ml) ground mace
1 tsp (5 ml) aniseed
1 tsp (5 ml) caraway seed
8 oz (225 g) flour

Beat the butter with the
rosewater, then cream with the
sugar. Mix in the beaten eggs and
spices, then work in the flour to
make a stiff dough. Make into
long rolls about ¼ inch (5 mm) in
diameter, and form into knots,
rings, or plaited strips before
baking on lightly greased baking
sheets for 15-20 minutes at gas
mark 4, 350°F (180°C).

Henry Fairfax: Arcana Fairfaxiana

MARZIPAN BACON

*To make Collops like Bacon of
Marchpane: Take some of your
Marchpane Paste and work it in red
Saunders till it be red: then rowl a
broad sheet of white Paste, and a sheet
of red Paste, three of the white, and
four of the red, and so one upon another
in mingled sorts, every red between,
then cut it overthwart, till it look like
Collops of Bacon, then dry it.*

8 oz (225 g) ground almonds
4 oz (100 g) caster sugar
2 tbls (30 ml) rosewater
red food colouring
cornflour or icing sugar for dusting

Beat the almonds and sugar with
the rosewater to form a stiff paste.
Divide in two, and knead a few
drops of the red food colour into
one half. Using either cornflour or
icing sugar to dust the paste, roll
out half the white mixture into a
rectangle about ⅜ inch (10 mm) in
thickness, and the remainder into
three thinner rectangles of the
same size. Divide the red paste
into four, and roll each piece out
into similar rectangles. Starting
with the thick white slab ('the fat')
build up alternate red and white
layers to form a miniature piece
of streaky bacon, from which thin
slices or 'collops' can then be cut
and allowed to dry.

*W.M.: The Compleat Cook and
Queen's Delight, 1671 edition*

SHROPSHIRE CAKES

To make a Shropsheere cake: Take two pound of dryed flour after it has been searced fine, one pound of good sugar dried and searced, also a little beaten sinamon or some nottmegg greeted and steeped in rose water; so straine two eggs, whites and all, not beaten to it, as much unmelted butter as will work it to a paste: so mould it & roule it into longe rouses, and cutt off as much at a time as will make a cake, two ounces is enough for one cake: then roule it in a ball between your hands; so flat it on a little white paper cut for a cake, and with your hand beat it about as big as a cheese trancher and a little thicker than a past board: then prick them with a comb not too deep in squares like diamons and prick the cake in every diamon to the bottom; so take them in a oven not too hot: when they rise up white let them soake a little, then draw. If the sugar be dry enough you need not dry it but searce it: you must brake in your eggs after you have wroat in some of your butter into your flower: prick and mark them when they are cold: this quantity will make a dozen and two or three, which is enough for my own at a time: take off the paper when they are cold.

8 oz (225 g) butter
1 lb (450 g) flour
8 oz (225 g) caster sugar
¼ tsp (1.5 ml) grated nutmeg
1 egg
1 tsp (5 ml) rosewater

Rub the butter into the dry ingredients, then work in the egg and rosewater to form a very stiff dough. Cut off lumps of dough, and work into ¼ inch (5 mm) thick cakes, 4 inches (10 cm) in diameter. Using a comb, mark the top surface into diamonds, cutting half-way through the cake, then use a broad skewer to prick through the centre of each diamond. Transfer to baking sheets, and bake for 20 minutes at gas mark 4, 350°F (180°C). Remove from the sheets with a metal spatula, and place on a wire tray to cool.

Madam Susanne Avery: A Plain Plantain

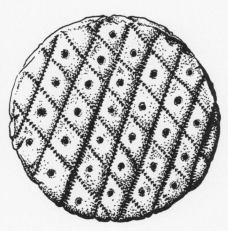

A Shropshire cake, marked with a comb and a skewer

SPICE CAKE

To make an Extraordinary Good Cake: Take half a bushel of the best flour you can get, very finely searced, and lay it on a large pastry board, make a hold in the middle thereof, put to it three pounds of the best butter you can get; with 14 pounds of currants finely picked and rubbed, three quarts of good new thick cream, 2 pounds of fine sugar beaten, 3 pints of new ale barm or yeast, 4 ounces of cinnamon beaten fine and searced, also an ounce of beaten ginger, 2 ounces of nutmegs beaten fine and searced; put in all these material together, and work them up to an indifferent stiff paste. Keep it warm till the oven be hot, then make it up and bake it, being baked an hour and a half ice it, then take 4 pounds of double refined sugar, beat it and searce it, and put it in a clean scowered skillet the quantity of a gallon, and boil it to a candy height with a little rosewater, then draw the cake, run it all over, and set it in the oven till it be candied.

3 oz (75 g) butter
1 lb (450 g) plain flour
12 oz (350 g) currants
2 oz (50 g) sugar
½ tsp (2.5 ml) ground cinnamon
½ tsp (2.5 ml) ground ginger
¼ tsp (1.5 ml) grated nutmeg
½ pt (275 ml) cream
½ oz (15 g) dried yeast mixed with
    1 tsp (5 ml) sugar and ¼ pt
    (150 ml) warm water

For glazing:
1 tbls (15 ml) sugar
1 tbls (15 ml) rosewater

Rub the butter into the flour, add the remainder of the dry ingredients, and mix in the cream and yeast to form a soft dough. Leave to rise in a warm place for about an hour, when it will double in size, then knead and place in a greased 8 inch (20 cm) cake tin. Leave to prove for 20 minutes, then bake at gas mark 7, 425°F (220°C) for 20 minutes, then for 1 hour at gas mark 5, 375°F (190°C). Melt the sugar in the rosewater over a low heat, and brush this glaze over the cake immediately after removing it from the oven.

Robert May: The Accomplisht Cook

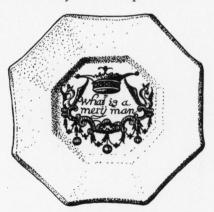

One of a set of six plates made in white tin-glazed earthenware decorated with purple and yellow brushwork. It was made in London in the 1680s

GINGERBREAD

To make Gingerbread: Take three stale Manchets and grate them, drie them, and sift them through a fine sieve, then adde unto them one ounce of ginger beeing beaten, and as much Cinamon, one ounce of liquorice and aniseedes being beaten together and searced, halfe a pound of sugar, then boile all these together in a posnet, with a quart of claret wine till they come to a stiffe paste with often stirring of it; and when it is stiffe, mold it on a table and so drive it thin, and print it in your moldes: dust your moldes with Cinamon, Ginger, and liquorice, beeing mixed together in fine powder. This is your gingerbread used at the Court, and in all gentlemens houses at festival times. It is otherwise called drie Leach.

8 oz (225 g) fresh white breadcrumbs
1 tsp (5 ml) ground ginger
1 tsp (5 ml) cinnamon
1 tsp (5 ml) aniseed
1 tsp (5 ml) ground liquorice (if
    available)
1 oz (25 g) sugar
¼ pt (150 ml) claret

Dry the breadcrumbs under the grill or in the oven (but without browning), and add to the remaining ingredients in a saucepan. Work the mixture over a gentle heat with a wooden spoon, until it forms a stiff dough. Turn the dough out on to a wooden board dusted with ground ginger and cinnamon and roll it out to about ¼ inch (5 mm) in thickness. It may then be impressed with a small stamp, a 1 inch (2.5 cm) diameter butter print being ideal for this purpose, and cut into small circles, using a pastry cutter. If antique gingerbread moulds are available, then they should be dusted with the ground spices before the slab of dough is firmly impressed into their designs. Then, after the surplus has been trimmed off with a knife, the gingerbread can be removed by inverting the moulds, and gently knocking their edges down on to the table.

Sir Hugh Platt: Delightes for Ladies

● Like most early gingerbreads, this version releases its flavours gradually, the gentle aniseed being slowly overwhelmed by the fiery ginger.

DEVONSHIRE WHITE POT

Take a pint of Cream and strain four Eggs into it, and put a little salt and a little sliced Nutmeg, and season it with sugar somewhat sweet, then take almost a penny Loaf of fine bread sliced very thin, and put it into a dish that will hold it, the Cream and the Eggs being put to it, then take a handfull of Raisins of the Sun being boiled, and a little sweet Butter, so bake it.

2 oz (50 g) raisins
1 lb (450 g) white bread, crusts
    removed and thinly sliced
1 oz (25 g) butter
3 eggs
1 pt (575 ml) single cream
¼ tsp (1.5 ml) grated nutmeg
¼ tsp salt
3 oz (75 g) sugar

Soak the raisins in hot water for 10 minutes. Line a 2 pint (1.1 litre) ovenproof dish with some of the the remainder, mixing in the raisins and knobs of the butter. Beat the eggs with the cream and stir in the nutmeg, salt and sugar. Pour over the bread, and allow it to stand for 15 minutes. Bake at gas mark 4, 350°F (180°C), for 40-50 minutes.

Rebecca Price: The Compleat Cook

QUAKING PUDDING

To make a quaking Pudding: Take a pint and somewhat more of thick Cream, ten Eggs, put the whites of three, beat them very well with two spoonfuls of Rose-water: mingle with your cream three spoonfuls of fine flour: mingle it so well, that there be no lumps in it, put it altogether, and season it according to your Tast: butter a Cloth very well, and let it be thick that it may not run out, and let it boyl for half an hour as fast as you can, then take it up and make Sauce with Butter, Rosewater and Sugar, and serve it up. You may stick some blanched Almonds upon it if you please.

4 egg yolks
2 egg whites
½ pt (275 ml) double cream
1½ tbls (25 ml) flour
1 tbls (15 ml) rosewater
butter
1 oz (25 g) blanched almonds, to
    decorate
For the sauce:
2 tbls (30 ml) rosewater
2 tbls (30 ml) sugar
2 oz (50 g) butter
2 tbls (30 ml) water

Beat the egg yolks and whites into the cream, then beat in the flour and rosewater to form a thick batter. Rub a piece of butter into a thick pudding cloth to help it to retain the batter. Support the cloth in a 1 pint (575 ml) basin, pour in the batter, tie the cloth securely, and plunge the pudding into a pan of boiling water. Simmer for 30 minutes, then remove from the pan, swiftly plunge in cold water, turn the pudding out on to a warm plate, and decorate with almonds. Make the sauce by melting the ingredients together, stirring constantly, and pour over the pudding.

Rebecca Price: The Compleat Cook

SYLLABUB

My Lady Middlesex makes Syllabubs for little Glasses with spouts, thus Take 3 pints of sweet Cream, one of quick white wine (or Rhenish), and a good wine glassful (better the ¼ of a pint) of Sack; mingle them with about three quarters of a pound of fine Sugar in Powder. Beat all these together with a whisk, till all appeareth converted into froth. Then pour it into your little Syllabub-glasses, and let them stand all night. The next day the Curd will be thick and firm above, and the drink clear under it. I conceive it may do well, to put into each glass (when you pour your liquor into it) a sprig of Rosemary a little bruised, or a little Lemon-peel, or some such thing to quicken the taste… or Nutmegs, or Mace, or Cloves, a very little.

1 pt (575 ml) double cream
7 fl oz (200 ml) Rhenish white wine
2 tbls (30 ml) dry sherry
4 oz (125 g) caster sugar
sprigs of rosemary or the peeled zest of a lemon

Beat the cream, wines and sugar together to form a thick froth, and spoon into large wine glasses. Insert the rosemary or lemon as desired, and allow to stand in a cool place for at least 12 hours before serving. The resulting syllabub is one of the most delicately flavoured, smooth and delicious of all seventeenth-century dishes.

Sir Kenelm Digby: The Closet of Sir Kenelm Digby Opened

Made by George Ravenscroft, this glass spouted vessel of 1677 was used for serving syllabub, the spout allowing the clear wine which collected beneath the creamy curd to be drunk separately

ORANGE BUTTER

*R. a quarter of a Pint of cleared juice of
Oranges, a quarter of a Pint of white
wine, pare the Peel of your Oranges
thinne, steep itt in the juice & white-
wine halfe an hour, then put in when
you have taken out the pill a little fine
Sugar, to take away the sharpnesse.
Then beat the yolks of six eggs very
well, & put them into the liquor, & sett
them over the fire, & keep itt
continually stirring till you find it almost
as thick as Butter then throw itt about
the dish or bason, & let itt stand all
night, in the morning take itt off lightlie
with a spoon, & serve itt as other
Butter.*

*¼ pt (150 ml) fresh orange juice, and
    thinly-peeled zest of the oranges
¼ pt (150 ml) white wine
6 egg yolks
2 tbls (30 ml) sugar*

Soak the zest in the orange juice
and white wine for 30 minutes, to
enrich the flavour, and then
remove. Beat the egg yolks and
sugar and add to the orange juice.
Pour the mixture into a saucepan,
and stir continuously over a low
heat until thick and creamy, but
do not allow to boil. Allow the
butter to cool and serve with
wafers as a rich full-flavoured
fruit dip.

*The Savile Recipe Book, 1683, quoted
in The Gentlewoman's Kitchen*

MARMALADE

*To make marmelade of Lemmons or
Oranges: Take ten Lemmons or
Oranges and boyle them with halfe a
dozen pippins, and so drawe them
through a strainer, then take so much
sugar as the pulp dooth weigh, and
bottle it as you doe Marmelade of
Quinces, and boxe it up.*

For 2 lb (900 g) marmalade use:
*5 large lemons (or oranges)
3 apples (Cox's pippins, for example)
¼ pt (150 ml) water
about 1 lb (450 g) sugar*

Cut the pointed ends off the
lemons, quarter them, and take
out the pips while holding them
over a stainless steel pan. Peel,
core, and quarter the apples, then
place them in the pan with the
lemons and water, cover and
simmer gently until tender –
about 45-60 minutes. Remove the
fruit from the heat and convert it
into a stiff pulp either by rubbing
it through a sieve with the back of
a wooden spoon, or by blending
it until smooth. Weigh the pulp,
transfer it into a clean saucepan
with its own weight of sugar, and
stir over a low heat until it boils to
setting point (221°F/105°C).
If it is to be stored for some time,
the marmalade may be packed
into glass jars and sealed in the
usual way, but if it is to be served
within the next day or so, it may

be either spooned into small waxed paper baking cases, or spread as a ½ inch (12 mm) thick slab on a sheet of waxed paper. It can then be cut into small cubes, sprinkled with caster sugar, and eaten with a fork.

Sir Hugh Platt: Delightes for Ladies

SACK POSSET

My Lord of Carlile's Sack-possett: Take a Pottle of Cream, and boil in it a little whole Cinnamon, and three or four flakes of Mace. To this proportion of Cream put in eighteen yolkes of Eggs, and eight of the whites; a pint of Sack. Beat your Eggs very well, and mingle them with your Sack, Put in three quarters of a pound of Sugar into the Wine and Eggs with a Nutmeg grated, and a little beaten Cinnamon; set the basin on the fire with the wine and Eggs, and let it be hot. Then put in the Cream boyling from the fire, pour it on high, but stir it not; cover it with a dish, and when it is settled, strew on the top a little fine Sugar mingled with three grains of Ambergreece and one grain of Musk and serve it up.

9 egg yolks
4 egg whites
½ pt (275 ml) dry sherry
¼ tsp (1.5 ml) cinnamon
¼ tsp (1.5 ml) ground mace
½ tsp (2.5 ml) grated nutmeg
2 pt (1.1/L) single cream
6 oz (175g) sugar

Beat together the egg yolks, egg whites, sherry and spices, and gently heat in a large pan, stirring constantly, until warm, but still not thickened. Heat the cream and sugar together and as it rises to the full boil pour from a good height into the warm eggs and sherry mixture. Allow the posset to stand in a warm place for a few minutes, sprinkle a little sugar across its surface, and serve.

Sir Kenelm Digby: The Closet of Sir Kenelm Digby Opened

The hollow stem of this 1690 wine glass contains a silver 6d. of William III

THE
ENGLISH
Houfe-Wife,

CONTAING

The inward and outward Vertues which
ought to be in a Compleat WOMAN.

As her Skill in *Phyfick,* *Chirurgery,* *Cookery,* Extraction of *Oyls,*
Banqueting ftuff, *Ordering of great Feafts,* Preferving *of all fort of*
Wides, *conceited Secrets,* *Diftillatians,* *Perfmes,* Ordering of *Wool,*
Hemp, *Flax:* Making *Cloth* and *Dying;* The knowledge of
Dayries : Office of *Malting;* of *Oats,* their excellent ufes in Fa-
milies : Of *Brewing,* *Baking,* and all other things belonging to an
Houfhold.

A *Work* generally approved, and now the
Eighth time much Augmented, Purged, and made moft
profitable and neceffary for all men, and the general good
of this NATION.

By *G. Markham.*

LONDON,
Printed for *George Sawbridge,* at the Sign of the *Bible* on
Ludgate Hill. 1675.

Title page, The English Housewife, *Markham, 1675*

BIBLIOGRAPHY

Anon, *The Second Book of Cookery* (London, 1641).

Anon, *A Book of Fruits & Flowers,* 1653, reprinted with an introduction by C. Anne Wilson, by Prospect Books (London, 1984).

Avery, Madam Susanne, *A Plain Plantain,* 1688 (Ditchling, Sussex, 1922).

Brears, P.C.D., *The Gentlewoman's Kitchen,* Wakefield Historical Publications (Wakefield, 1984).

Cromwell, Elizabeth (Joan), *The Court and Kitchen of Mrs Elizabeth Commonly called Joan Cromwell,* 1664, reprinted by Cambridgeshire Libraries (Cambridge, 1983).

Digby, Sir Kenelm, *The Closet of Sir Kenelm Digby Opened,* 1669 (London, 1910).

Driver, C., and Berridale-Johnson, M., *Pepys at Table,* Bell and Hyman (London, 1984)

Evelyn, John, *Acetaria, a Discourse of Sallets,* 1699, reprinted by Prospect Books (London, 1982).

Fairfax, Henry, and others, *Arcana Fairfaxiana,* mid 17th century (Newcastle, 1890).

May, Robert, *The Accomplisht Cook* (London, 1660).

Mosley, Jane, *Jane Mosley's Derbyshire Recipes 1669–1712,* Derbyshire Museums Service (Derby, 1979).

Murrel, J., *A New Booke of Cookerie,* 1615, reprinted by Da Capo Press (New York, 1972).

Platt, Sir Hugh, *Delightes for Ladies To adorne their Persons, Tables, Closets, and Distillatories with Beauties, Banquets, Perfumes and Waters,* printed by Humferey Lownes (London, 1608).

Price, Rebecca, *The Compleat Cook,* 1681, Routledge and Kegan Paul (London, 1974).

W.M., *The Compleat Cook and Queen's Delight,* 1671 edn. reprinted by Prospect Books (London, 1984).

Early seventeenth-century supper party

RECIPE INDEX

Illustration acknowledgements:

Mary Evans Picture Library, *Roxburghe Collection, British Museum,* frontispiece, 42.
Michael Holford, *London Coffee House,* cover.